Seeking the Swilly

a story of the Londonderry & Lough Swilly Railway and its Bus Services

Hugh Dougherty

Two local gents contemplate life outside Marners, the Swilly bus agency in Carndonagh, as number 215, an ex-Willowbrook bodied, Leyland Leopard, ex-Trent Motor Services, waits to leave for Derry in July 1981..
Hugh Dougherty

© Hugh Dougherty, 2024
First published in the United Kingdom, 2024,
by Stenlake Publishing Ltd.
54-58 Mill Square, Catrine, KA5 6RD
www.stenlake.co.uk
ISBN 978-1-84033-980-2

The publishers regret that they cannot supply copies of any pictures featured in this book.

Printed by
P2D Books, 1 Newlands Rd,
Westoning, Bedford, MK45 5LD

OUR OLD LOUGH SWILLY BUS

She came down from Derry
Rocking and rolling, too
Calling at Letterkenny, lifting passengers anew
By Barnes Gap and Termon the Swilly bus did go
Threading Donegal's wild Highlands, for Creeslough and Dungloe
She carried papers, parcels, mails, chickens (!) – locals, too
Folk for Falcarragh and Kinasslagh, where passengers were few
She brought Scotchies home for holidays and took them back again
Just the ticket for the Rosses, descended from the Swilly train
Luggage piled high on the roof by conductors with great fuss
But now she's gone forever, our old Lough Swilly bus

Hugh Dougherty 2024

The LSR diamond as worn by steam locomotives on their side-tanks and company lorries. *Hugh Dougherty*

The LS logo in use in the 1980s. *Hugh Dougherty*

SEEKING THE SWILLY - Early Days

I was fascinated by the County Donegal Railways as a teenager on holidays in ancestral Donegal, but I have to admit, that the Londonderry & Lough Swilly Railway, the county's other narrow gauge marvel, and the CDR's great rival, came a close second. The fact that the Dougherty family originates in Innishowen, deep within Swilly territory, might have something to do with that. Just don't tell any of the readers of my book on the CDR bus services!

My parents gave me a copy of EM Patterson's history of the L&LSR as a present in 1964, and, on holidays in Glenties each year, we'd drive north, over the Gweebarra Bridge to Dungloe, Burtonport and the Rosses. That's when I began to see plenty of the then current Swilly bus and lorry operations, as well as the intriguingly abandoned track of the Letterkenny & Burtonport Extension Railway. I had to find out more, my Swilly search was on!

There was a wild beauty and romanticism about the land the railway traversed, coupled to the indefinable, magical appeal of the narrow gauge, and there was a link with Glasgow, too. Older neighbours would tell me that they had boarded the Swilly train at Gweedore, Crolly or Dungloe Road, escaping poverty and land hunger, to rattle off to Derry on the hard, wooden, seats of their 3ft gauge carriage, for the 'The Scotch Boat' and a new life on Clydeside. Later arrivals from the emigrations of the 50s and 60s, would fondly recall catching the Lough Swilly bus that had replaced the trains. No surprise, then, that this unique railway company, founded as early as 1853, and, without a train to its name for the last 59 years of its existence, but definitely, still a RAILWAY company (!), caught my youthful imagination.

In 1965, when I was 14, we drove up to Letterkenny, where I marvelled at the Swilly's station, sited, cheek-by-jowl, with the CDR's own. Both, though devoid of narrow gauge rails, were still in use for bus passengers and road freight, while

Gaeltacht-bound at Letterkenny Station in July 1965, is Leyland Royal Tiger, number 72, its roof rack packed with Irish language students' bikes. A lad hangs out of a window, eyeing a passenger absorbed in his *Irish Independent* and his choc ice as he waits for the Derry bus. *Hugh Dougherty*

the Lough Swilly had a maintenance shed for lorries and buses, too. I wanted to linger longer to unearth what was left of the railway, which enjoyed such continuity with the company's then grey and green-liveried buses and lorries. The lorries, delivering goods throughout north and west Donegal, as successors to the trains, proudly bore the LSR diamond logo, formerly carried by steam engines, emblazoned on their cab doors.

But, the parents were keen to push on to scenic Downings, where my mother's *clann*, the McBrides, originated, so I reluctantly left the station, complete with ex-CDR Baltic tank, *Erne*, lying in the yard, kindly repainted in green by the Swilly folk. Its livery initially fooled me into believing that it was an LSR loco, which was then, hopefully, awaiting export to the United Sates as part of the ill-fated Dr Ralph Cox narrow gauge railway scheme there. That never happened and *Erne* was broken up in 1969, some parts, according to local legend, being buried under the surface of the yard, now part of today's Bus Eireann depot.

The very active ghost of the CDR and Lough Swilly trains still hung about Letterkenny, and, despite the rails being gone, the stations still had the air of an operating frontier, just as the celebrated narrow gauge writer and explorer, JIC Boyd, described, when he took the train to a then, very remote, Burtonport, in 1939. After taking a quick picture of Leyland Royal Tiger 72, stuffed with kids heading for the Gaeltacht summer colleges, complete with bikes and suitcases on the on the roof rack, in the best traditions of the company, I resolved to return again.

If at all possible, I imagined taking a Londonderry & Lough Swilly Railway bus, to Burtonport, an epic journey, in my young mind. The bus did the 74 miles in just under four hours, and no faster than the railway timetable of the 1920s. I may have missed the Letterkenny and Burtonport trains by 32 years, but, at least, I wouldn't miss the replacement bus!

We drove on, through wild and remote Barnes Gap, complete with then very visible remains of the Burtonport line's viaduct, cuttings and embankments. I even managed to persuade my father to divert off the main road and stop long enough for me to drink in the remains of the Owencarrow Viaduct. There, on 30th January 1925, a train had been blown off the bridge by a fierce Atlantic gale, killing four passengers, injuring several more, and earning the railway worldwide headlines of the wrong sort.

The viaduct location was, and remains, a bleak spot, and I could imagine the stricken train, that fateful night, hauled by 4-6-2 tank number 14, creeping across the seemingly spindly viaduct, dwarfed by the wild grandeur of the Donegal Highlands. A verbatim description of the accident by the fireman, 25 year-old Johnny Hannigan, brought it all to life. I was driven by the enthusiasm of youth, to unearth more in those pre-internet days, when it took determination and effort to discover facts, rather than, as today, via the screen of a mobile phone, on which pictures, facts and figures

The Lough Swilly engine that wasn't! County Donegal Railways 4-6-4T *Erne*, in Letterkenny Station yard in July 1965, fooling Hugh into believing that it was a Swilly loco as it had been repainted in Lough Swilly green.
Hugh Dougherty

Number 72, mysteriously parked, deep in CDR territory at Donegal Diamond, in July 1965. *Hugh Dougherty*

Dungloe's Driver Sweeney and the Falcarragh agent, dressed in civvies, have parked their bus at Killybegs Station in August 1965, while their passengers enjoyed the town's annual sea angling festival.
Hugh Dougherty

about the Swilly, and every other railway in the world, tumble forth at the touch of a finger. It was a very different world.

As luck would have it, we took a drive, one fine July evening, all the way up to the Rosses, and as far north as Gweedore, where, at the site of the old station, which I had persuaded the father to stop at, with his usual moans, to allow me to inspect the then, still-extant buildings and water tower, I met the Swilly's agent, a Mr Anthony Delap, who lived in the station house.

He turned out to be the former station master, now the Lough Swilly's bus inspector for the area, and said that it was a tragedy the line had closed. He fired my imagination further by relating tales of special trains, of the War of Independence and Civil War's considerable impact on the railway, and, of course the Owencarrow Viaduct disaster. "You should look up Johny Hannigan," he told me. "He lives in Letterkenny and still works for us on lorry maintenance. Just ask for him at the station. He'll be happy to talk to you." That was a tall order for a wee boy like me, but I filed it away for future reference.

At Letterkenny Station, I'd picked up a copy of the company's bus timetable, and what a delight it was. The cover, depicting an artist's impression of one of the Swilly's, characteristic Leyland Royal Tigers, running through the hills of Donegal, contained timetables for all the routes, railway replacement and other services alike, proudly headed "L&LS Rly- Bus Services". There were connections listed with the CDR buses and Ulster Transport Authority trains for Belfast and Dublin. This was a well-integrated transport company, even offering through railway fares by UTA trains, a three month, through return from Belfast to Burtonport, train to Derry and Swilly bus onwards, being listed at 64/5 in 1964. Like their County Donegal Railways counterparts, LSR conductors had plenty to do handling through rail tickets, as well as coping with mails, parcels and newspapers. The job was no sinecure, despite being steady, reasonably well paid for a rural area, and with the perks of a free uniform and travel concessions.

And, a selection of supporting adverts in the timetable included one for the Burns-Laird Line and its all-important 'Scotch Boat' to

The L&LSRly bus timetable that enticed the author to seek the Swilly, an intriguing railway company without a train!   *Hugh Dougherty collection*

Glasgow, a major source of traffic for the Swilly, carrying seasonal 'tattie howkers' to and from Scotland, returning exiles, and young folk emigrating, as well as cattle and freight.

And, talking of the Scotch Boat, known, quite logically, as the Derry Boat among Donegal exiles in Glasgow (!), I can well recall a visit to Derry on the last day of the Glasgow Fair Holidays in 1965. I caught sight of what seemed to be practically the whole Swilly bus fleet, drawn up at the quayside, beside MV *Lairds Loch*, having brought returning crowds of exiles from all across the railway's territory to the boat.

Stressed-out conductors and drivers were shinning up the rear ladders of the single deckers, emptying the roof racks of suitcases, while the Scotchies, as they were known to the crews, sorted them on the quayside. Many had braved the dreaded customs at Bridgend and Killea, on the way back into the north, and several were unwrapping bales of Donegal tweed that they'd wound round themselves and hidden under their outer garments, to avoid import duty! If only I had brought my camera that day…

But, back to the timetable booklet, which came complete with a service map, Lough Swilly tide tables, and a timetable for Brown Bros of Inch Island. They operated ferry services on the Lough, and bought the marine operations from the Swilly in 1952, so ending the company's claim to fame of being a railway, bus, lorry and shipping company, and much more than just a mere narrow gauge railway!

That wee, green, booklet fired my imagination, and I spent many hours working out journeys for when I'd have enough pocket money and maybe even be able to persuade the parents into allowing 14-year-old me to take a solo, trip, into the fastness of the Rosses, despite the fact that the Swilly operated in territory quite far from our Glenties base, firmly in CDR land.

A Swilly bus, mysteriously parked in Donegal Diamond one day, deep in CDR territory, only whetted my appetite for more, as did a LSR bus parked outside Killybegs Station, as its passengers enjoyed the delights of the town's Sea Angling Festival. Tours and excursions were a big part of the Swilly's business.

In the meantime, I'd glean what I could from the parental car. Often we'd take a Sunday trip to the fine strand at Magheraroarty. There, you'd find a Lough Swilly Leyland Royal Tiger, just like the one on the timetable cover, parked up on the dunes, while its passengers, boys and girls from the Gaeltacht college, all staying in Donegal for the summer to learn Irish, rioted happily – in Engligh it has to be said (!) – on the beach, as the driver, in full uniform, enjoyed a snooze on the Machar beside vehicle. Lough Swilly buses were like that: you found them parked up in surprisingly remote spots, especially as crews took them home with them at the end of a shift, saving dead mileage, and working in next morning to Letterkenny and Derry where docking was done.

And, talking of Irish, Lough Swilly staff had to be fluent in

Gweedore Station was fairly intact in July 1975, with water tower, goods shed and platform waiting shelter, looking towards Burtonport.
Hugh Dougherty

English, Derry dialect, as spoken by the famous *Derry Girls*, Ulster Scots around Newton and Manorcunningham, Irish in the Gaeltacht areas of Gweedore, the Rosses and Clonmany, and Glaswegian, when the Scotchies swarmed off the boat in Derry! The Swilly was a multilingual company.

Best of all, for a keen youngster like me, the Swilly was staffed by people who were pleased to find that you were interested in their trains, buses and lorries, that they ran as much like a railway as they could, and very consciously, too, of traditions of the company, which ran its first train in 1863, with its headquarters over the border in Derry, but running nearly all its traffic miles in the Republic.

Much more than a mere road transport company, the L&LSR was very much part of the life of the communities of north and west Donegal. From the 1960s, when its buses and lorries were bustling and profitable, through to the sad demise of the company in 2014, the result of diminishing traffic over three decades, rising car ownership rates, increasing competition from independent operators, and the coup de gras of an Inland Revenue unpaid tax bill, caused it to cease operations after 151 years. Eighty staff lost their jobs and Donegal lost its last, active link with the great days of its narrow gauge railways, the Swilly going the same way as its great rival, the County Donegal Railways Joint Committee, taken over by CIE in 1971.

This short book tells how I've sought out and experienced the Swilly, which, now, 71 years after its last train ran in 1953, nearly a century after the Owencarrow disaster, and a decade since the last Swilly bus operated, continues to be remembered with affection by the communities it served so faithfully. That was very much despite the harsh realities of the financial and political world the company operated in, especially after partition put a border, with all the operational difficulties that it brought, firmly in the Swilly's way.

Remarkably, the Londonderry & Lough Swilly Railway, to give the company its full title, continues to be sought out and rediscovered, and, if you look around north and west Donegal,

Burtonport Station, terminus of the Swilly's, epic 74-mile journey from Derry, was still there in August 1974. *Hugh Dougherty*

you'll find a fascinating amount surviving, and, as we'll see, even being restored today. My own Swilly search goes on, and there's always something new to discover.

I hope that you will enjoy reading of how I sought and continue to seek out this unique, Irish railway institution, which first caught my interest six decades ago. The Swilly left lasting social and economic benefits in north and west Donegal, as well as establishing and maintaining vital links between Glasgow and my ancestral homeland. What a pity it's not still with us, today.

You'd meet a Lough Swilly bus on the L&BER replacement service, still taking four hours from Derry. A busy, Dungloe-bound, Royal Tiger, 77, picks up passengers near Gweedore in August 1973.
Hugh Dougherty

SEEKING THE SWILLY – THE HERO OF THE OWENCARROW

The Owencarrow Viaduct, gingerly carrying the Burtonport line across the great defile, a continuation of Scotland's Great Glen, between Kilmacrennan and Creeslough, in the wild, fastness of the Donegal Highlands, had long caught my interest and imagination. I'd remembered Anthony Delap at Gweedore Station telling me, away back in 1965, that Johnny Hannigan, fireman on the ill-fated train that was blown off the bridge in January 1925, still worked for the railway in Letterkenny. I'd resolved to track him down.

So, I caught the CDR bus in Glenties on a July day in 1967, changed at Ballybofey for Strabane, and arrived in Letterkenny via the bus from Strabane, retracing the route of the Strabane & Letterkenny Railway, and clutching my CDR booklet timetable in case I got stranded on such a long journey! Distances seemed greater in those days. I had also been entrusted with my big sister's Brownie 126 camera, borrowed for the occasion, containing a precious Ilford, colour 'spool' of just eight frames, saved up for with grim determination, as were the bus fares.

I got talking to the driver, on the journey up from Strabane to Letterkenny. He turned out to be Michael Gallen, a genuine, former, CDR railcar motorman, who had stories in plenty of the Strabane & Letterkenny railway. You could touch the atmosphere as well as his regret that the railway had been closed just eight years before.

As soon as we stopped at Letterkenny CDR Station, which still boasted its platform canopy, a covered van, used for storage, in the

The Owencarrow Disaster: the rescue train from Derry, hauled by one of the 4-8-4 tank locos, sits on the viaduct behind the stricken carriages.
Donegal Railway Heritage Museum

Letterkenny Station was still in use for buses and lorries when I met Johnny Hannigan. The station house and building are intact and the Leyland Royal Tiger is standing where the track and trains used to be, while a former railway carriage moulders in the background. *Hugh Dougherty*

bay platform, working goods shed, a refreshment room, and, of course, 4-6-4T *Erne*, in the yard, I asked Michael where best to find Johnny Hannigan. "Ye'll get him down at the Swilly," he replied, pointing to the adjacent station building, a dead ringer for Glenties Station on the CDR, and Carndonagh on the Swilly, too, and wished me all the best.

Now, as a seasoned journalist, I've interviewed hundreds of the great and the good over the last four decades, but, as a 16 year-old still at school, this was new territory. Think back to yourself at that age. Why would a teenage boy want to interview an 'old' man about the past? Would he think I was mad? Suppose he wasn't around? Had I wasted my hard-saved cash? And I'd better watch my time in case I missed the return CDR bus. Glenties seemed an awful long way away from Letterkenny! And that was not forgetting a cast-iron sign beside the Swilly bus and lorry maintenance shed which read "L&LSR TRESPASSERS PROSECUTED".

But by that time, I was at the Swilly booking office in the station building, its floor strewn with parcels traffic for the buses, and a man in traditional railway uniform told me that Johhny Hannigan was around. "Just go down to the engine shed there, and you'll find him, son." Obstacle one over.

I was still nervous as I walked along the platform and past the goods shed, avoiding Swilly lorries loading, and passed a grounded Letterkenny & Burtonport Extension Railway coach beside the station building. And there was the loco shed, looking just as it always had done, but without track. By the water tower, a man in overalls, and wearing a cloth cap, was working on the rear wheel of a green-liveried Lough Swilly lorry trailer.

Summoning up all my courage, I asked him if he was Mr Hannigan. "Aye," he replied in a Donegal blast. "I am."

Hesitatingly, I told him I was interested in the railway and he quickly said: "So ye want me to tell you about the Owencarrow, then," and he laid down his tools, lit a Sweet Afton cigarette, leaned on the trailer, and began to tell me about the incident as if it was yesterday. He had total recall and a tear glinted in his eyes as he told of the deaths, that fateful night.

A daunting 'no trespassing' sign didn't put me off going past the Swilly Leyland Comet lorry to seek out the hero of the Owencarrow!

Hugh Dougherty

Johnny Hannigan, many years after the Owencarrow.
Hugh Dougherty collection.

"It was wild," he said. "Maybe we shouldn't have gone ahead from Kilmacrennan, but we didn't expect the train to be lifted by the wind as we'd had worse gales at the spot. It was a tragedy," he said, with a faraway look in his eye, clearly recalling heroically saving lives, helping the injured, and, then, walking, buffeted by the unforgiving gale, along the pitch-dark track to raise the alarm with the Creeslough station master, two hard miles distant.

And he began to talk at length about the Burtonport line. "Yes, I fired number 12, the big tender engine, and the big tanks, numbers 5 and 6, too, on that road. They had massive fireboxes and were hard work, but they could get ye to Burtonport without having to stop for coal. But the best engines were the wee tanks, numbers 1 to 4, they were the best running ones we had."

Johnny, I was, of course, calling him Mr Hannigan, as you did in those days, also had a tale about battles with the Board of Trade inspectors. "They used to pull us up for marshalling wagons in front of coaches, or for going downhill too hard," he recalled, clearly still annoyed at officialdom. But his best tale was of the time he was firing on an eight-coach special excursion train on which the locomotive, number 5 or 6, one of the big 4-8-4 tanks built specially for the Burtonport road, nearly failed in the middle of nowhere, far from fitters, with leaking boiler tubes.

"We had a heavy church pilgrimage special going from Burtonport to Kilmacrennan with pilgrims for Doon Well," he recalled, "and she failed with leaking tubes, on the way back in the middle of the bogs near Cashelnagor. Bob McGuinness, the driver, and I managed to raise enough pressure to crawl home, but by the time we got back to Burtonport it was nearly 9.00 o'clock on the Sunday morning. We had been due in at 11.00 pm on the Saturday night, but at least we got everyone back in time for Mass on the Sunday, although the passengers weren't exactly pleased!"

I was writing furiously to get all of this down, but my nerve failed, to my lasting regret, when it came to asking Mr Hannigan to pose for a picture, especially as we had talked for over an hour, and I didn't want to miss the CDR bus back to Strabane, and, eventually, Glenties. The parents would have gone crackers if I hadn't made it back. He slipped in a quick last word picture of carrying out the sad duty of driving the lifting train up to the Owencarrow in 1949, after the line closed, and I only wished that I could have stayed on a little longer. Johnny's lorry trailer repair could clearly wait for another day.

So, I thanked Mr Hannigan and headed home on Michael Gallen's CDR bus, chatting to him about my wonderful interview with Johhny. "He's a grand man," said Michael. "We're all railwaymen, and, like all of us, he misses the trains."

And miss them Johnny Hannigan did. He was 66 when I had the privilege of speaking to him at Letterkenny and he died some years later, but I was very glad that I had had the courage, or, youthful cheek, if you want, to seek him out and hear at first hand of his experiences of the Owencarrow Viaduct disaster, after which he received a commendation for his bravery that night.

Number 12, the big, 4-8-0 tender engine, making up its train at Burtonport, before setting off, calling at Cashelnagor and crossing the Owencarrow Viaduct, before reaching Derry after 74 epic miles.
Stenlake Publishing

The memorial, erected by local people, recalls the tragedy. *Hugh Dougherty*

Today, the spot that I met such an interesting Swilly engineman, is buried under a shopping centre, following the sale of the Swilly station in the 1980s, and even the company buses have passed into history. But, I can still, in my mind's eye, see a slightly awkward young lad, fired with the gauche enthusiasm of youth, talking to an older man who spoke softly, and who looked, from time to time, far away down the remains of the Burtonport line track bed, now buried under the tarmac of an inevitable new road. It was a journey back into a lost era of narrow gauge railway travel in Donegal, as I searched that day, now so long ago, for the Swilly.

Today, you can seek out a tasteful and moving memorial to the disaster, just near the Creeslough end of the bridge. It was commissioned and unveiled by the local community in 2021. With the centenary of the tragedy approaching in 2025, plans are being laid to mark that event which so shocked the country and community, and which made international headlines, just as the equally shocking Creeslough gas explosion tragedy did in October 2022, 97 years after the terrible events on the Owencarrow Viaduct that stormy January night.

If you're in Donegal, be sure to visit the Owencarrow memorial and view the remains of the bridge. It's a spot full of atmosphere and a reminder of the great forces of nature that the builders and operators of the Letterkenny & Burtonport line faced throughout its lifetime, as it battled through some of the most scenic but remote parts of the Donegal Highlands, under the shadows of Muckish and Errigal, in all of their Derryveagh Mountain splendour.

The remains of the viaduct beyond, marching across the valley.

Hugh Dougherty

A busy Letterkenny on the day I travelled with Leyland Leopard 136 having arrived from Derry via Killea. My ex-CDR, now CIE, Leyland Leopard, sits in the yard behind.
Hugh Dougherty

SEEKING THE SWILLY – IN THE TROUBLES

It's Monday 31st July, 1974, and I'm on holiday with my parents at Ballykillowen. Patricia, my fiancée had come over for the first two weeks of July, but now she's back in Glasgow and phoning her from pre-dial Donegal is a trial of sanity. The switchboard lady in Laghey Post Office knows we're missing one another! And so does most of the townland…

I'd always wanted to visit the Swilly's Pennyburn HQ in Derry, meaning a trip over the former County Donegal Railways, CIE, routes from Laghey to Letterkenny, and a Swilly bus from there into the Maiden City.

But, there was an ulterior motive, as they had dial phones in Derry – remember the days before mobiles! I could phone my wife-to-be, easily, seek out Pennyburn, the company's holy-of-holies, its HQ, since its earliest days as a broad gauge railway, meet the boss, take some pictures, get back home the same day, and flog the resulting article to *Buses* magazine.

So, I wrote off, asking to visit Pennyburn, and was replied to on genuine Londonderry & Lough Swilly Railway letterhead, signed by the general manager, RK Hamilton. It granted permission, and I was quite surprised that I was given the green light given all the turmoil in Derry.

Going from Donegal to Derry, in those days, by bus, was an adventure, not because CIE and Lough Swilly didn't run efficiently, but because crossing the border meant British Army checks. Coming from the Republic, being 23, having a name and face like mine, were all possible problems, but, as a young buck, there was the added attraction of a frisson of danger!

Off, then, on the 11.00 Sligo – Derry service to Ballybofey on a CIE 'C' Class Leopard, a bus whose airbag suspension wasn't wonderful on then-rough Donegal roads. The C bus never had been a great favourite with local crews, all of whom were either former Great Northern Railway of Ireland or CDR men, some of whom were ex-railcar drivers turned busmen, who swore by GNR Gardners, AECs, or the sturdy and reliable, CIE E Class Leopard.

We duly arrived at Ballybofey at 11.35 with the connection leaving, in the shape of a trusty CIE E Class Leopard, for Letterkenny at 11.40, so I had no time to drop in at the old CDR depot at Stranorlar. But, with the CIE bus due into Letterkenny at 12.25, and the Swilly connection to Derry not away until 13.25, I would have time to see the former CDR and L&LSR stations, both still giving sterling service as bus stations.

At Letterkenny, there were ex-CIE Leopards, transferred to the Swilly, as part of an Irish Government rescue operation, given the fact that the company was nearly bankrupt. Rumours were rife that the Swilly was about to shut up shop or be taken over by CIE, with the

Top deck view on the then-narrow main road from Letterkenny to Derry as we pass a Leopard on the long haul to Burtonport. *Hugh Dougherty*

After its army checkpoint ordeal, our steed enjoys a wash up at Pennyburn yard.
Hugh Dougherty

joint fleet being maintained at Stranorlar, a double irony as the depot was once the HQ of the County Donegal Railways, the LSR's great rival and sworn enemy!

The Troubles just over the border in Derry hadn't helped either, but talking to Swilly staff, I got the impression that morale wasn't too bad, and that the company's summer-only express service to and from Glasgow, operated jointly with Western SMT, via the Stranraer – Larne ferry, to replace the direct connection to Glasgow, lost after the Derry Boat was taken off in 1966, was doing quite well in the circumstances.

Letterkenny was the hub of the Lough Swilly system in 1974, with services going to Derry, Churchill, Burtonport, Fanad, Dungloe, Rosapenna and Downings, most routes still having three out and back journeys, some with a Sunday service, too. Conductors, mail, newspapers and parcels traffic, were still much in evidence.

But, behind the scenes, the company was really fighting for survival, battling an upsurge in car ownership in Donegal, the near collapse of tourism because of the Troubles, and fierce competition from local operators, many poaching traffic from the Swilly on the lucrative Donegal – Glasgow run.

Manager Ronnie Hamilton was juggling keeping the service going with a fleet that included the classic, Swilly bus, Saro-bodied, Leyland Royal Tigers, straight off the timetable covers, and dating from 1953, while imploring both the Dublin and Stormont Governments for aid, something that the company had been doing for a large part of its history, stretching back to railway-only days.

All that was at the back of my mind as I noticed some ex-CIE Leyland Leopards, sprayed in the Swilly's then new brownish-red and cream, 'zig-zag' livery, and on hire to the company from the Republic's national operator. This was aid-in-kind from the Dublin Government, to keep the wheels turning, especially as the L&LSR was responsible for school transport in its area.

My look around, including finding two Letterkenny & Burtonport Extension Railway coach bodies and the engine shed and water tower, all cementing the distinctive 'railway' atmosphere, finished when one of the Royal Tigers bounced into the dusty, station yard. The bus had covered the Burtonport line's route, leaving Dungloe at 10.00 am, and arriving in Letterkenny at 13.30, to almost the same timings as the trains.

A few passengers, including one besuited man, with suitcase, clambered aboard Derry-bound double decker, Leyland PD3, number 68, a 1959-built, Roe-bodied, 72-seater, acquired by the Swilly from Kippax & District in 1968. Typical of the used buses that the Swilly bought from UK operators, it worked the Derry – Letterkenny, Derry – Buncrana, and Derry – Moville routes, until withdrawn in 1982.

The conductor, a student on for the summer, issued my 0.83p excursion ticket, using his vintage, insert Setright machine, converted to decimal currency in 1971, and, as Sterling and Irish cash mingled freely around the Border, before Euros, the Swilly wasn't yet hit by the inconvenience and expense of operating in a two-currency area.

We shot along the then-narrow, Derry main road, enjoying views of Lough Swilly itself, not forgetting the Dougherty Castle at Burt (!), from my top-deck seat, and passed an ex-CIE, E Class, Leopard, heading for the fastness of Dungloe, over the same route as the train took to Burtonport, its conductor on the front platform, ready for parcels, mails and newspapers, all of which made up a substantial part of the company's revenue in those far-off days.

All went well until Killea, just outside Derry, for there was a British Army checkpoint, sited strategically, to search traffic coming into Derry from Donegal. The gun-toting soldiers brusquely ordered everyone off, with all the young men, me included, lined up alongside, pushed in the back, legs kicked apart, and made to balance against the bus lower deck panels, on finger tips.

The driver was told gruffly, to get out his cab and the young conductor's waybill was ripped up and tossed into the bushes. I was spun round, and a sergeant, flicking through a series of photographs of suspects, aggressively demanded my ID.

I produced my driving licence, with its Glasgow address, and that was enough to send him, from a Scottish regiment, into a tirade of anti-Irish invective. "A Glasgow Fenian on a bus from Donegal!" he screamed. "Wait there!"

So, I stood with the others as the Leyland diesel engine turned over, rhythmically, with comfortingly familiar sounds in a tense situation, while the driver lit up a philosophical fag. He anticipated a long wait. The suited man from Gweedore, who was carrying his even-then, old fashioned, suitcase, had also attracted attention.

He told the sergeant that he was catching the Belfast train at Derry to make the boat at Larne for Stranraer, and the train for Glasgow. That was enough for the soldier to decide that the bus could sit at Killea long enough to ensure that this man missed his train. Eventually, after a tense eternity, we were allowed to go, but not before the troops had ascertained, by radio, that I was not Hugh Doherty of the IRA, later involved in the Balcombe Street siege, who nearly shared my spelling of the clan name, and, more confusingly still, had grown up not far from my parents' house in Glasgow. Phew!

The PD3, surged thankfully forward, and the conductor, who was clearly well-used to having his waybill ripped up by the troops, lifted the long seat by the door, and triumphantly produced a copy. That was what Swilly crews had to do in those days to keep the service running.

Whenever I arrived at Pennyburn, courtesy of a lift up the Strand Road on a LSR road tanker, I met Ronnie Hamilton, who very honestly explained the difficulties that the company faced, and spoke of coming timetable rationalisation and a cost-cutting conversion to one man operation. Despite the Troubles, and, Derry was still reeling from the effects of Bloody Sunday of 1972, which had largely destroyed the Swilly's traffic in Donegal shoppers coming into the city, he vowed that the company would carry on as long as it could. "We're here to serve the people of the area we cover, despite all the difficulties we face," said Mr Hamilton, confidently. He was right, for the Swilly buses struggled on for another 40 years.

He presented me with some Setright insert tickets as a souvenir, and left me to photograph around the yard, the highlight of which was the former railway repair shops, with buses standing over pits lined by three foot gauge track rails, as though an engine might arrive at any minute. The Swilly was always more than just a bus company. It was definitely the Londonderry & Lough Swilly RAILWAY Company, as Mr Hamilton pointed out.

Around the yard, there was a variety of buses, ranging from our steed from Letterkenny, now going through the wash, a CIE C class Leopard in Swilly colours, to a variety of Atlanteans and other assorted second-hand vehicles from Scotland and England. I snapped away happily with my trusted Instamatic.

When it was time to get back to the bus station, to catch the CIE Derry-Galway express service, for Donegal Town, I let the office know I was away. "Hold on," said Mr Hamilton. "We've a bus going down to take up service to Letterkenny. I'll get the driver to take you."

So, standing beside the driver on the platform of his Saunders-Roe-bodied, Leyland Tiger Cub, which I seem to remember as number 71, bought new in 1951, we were halfway down the busy Strand Road, chatting about the Lough Swilly, which the driver had served for 25 years, when an armoured car shot past and screeched to a stop in front of us.

Out of the vehicle poured six, armed soldiers, who screamed at the driver to open that door, and dragged me off into the roadway. "Why the **** were you taking pictures of our base?" one screamed in my face. "Identity. Now."

So, I took out my driving licence, which, again, didn't help with its Irish name and Glasgow address, and they demanded my camera. Getting more worried, I produced Mr Hamilton's letter and against

Pennyburn was the Swilly holy of holies, as carried on all buses and their legal lettering. And, yes, it was a RAILWAY! *Hugh Dougherty*

Buses were still overhauled in the old locomotive works, complete with 3ft gauge track! *Hugh Dougherty*

There was plenty to photograph, with an ex-CIE C class Leyland Leopard passed to the Swilly as aid-in-kind. *Hugh Dougherty*

Pennyburn yard held plenty of variety that August day, so much so, that I didn't notice the army HQ in the background…. *Hugh Dougherty*

shouting and racist insults that were flying, managed to say that I had been taking pictures of the buses and had permission to do so. It then dawned on me that across the road from Pennyburn, was the British Army's Derry HQ. I was so busy seeking the Swilly and taking pictures that I had failed to clock that!

Following some radio traffic, the squaddies calmed down, threw my camera back at me without a word, disappeared into their Saracen, and shot off back up the Strand Road. The Swilly driver just shrugged. "It's like this all the time," he said. "You're lucky that you weren't arrested and taken away for questioning." Imagine explaining that to the parents and the fiancée!

It was with some relief that I boarded the Donegal-bound bus at Derry. As luck would have it, I knew the driver, who said he'd drop me off at Laghey, even though it wasn't a scheduled stop, and it was wonderful to cross the border into the relaxed home county. Even the rough riding of the C bus didn't worry me. It was good not to be in the cells, under interrogation, just because I was seeking out the Swilly!

What I had experienced, 50 years ago, was an insight into providing bus services at one of the worst of times in Derry. The effects of the Troubles, combined with the general rise in car ownership and the increasing challenges of providing rural bus services in the 1970s, experienced by all operators throughout the British Isles, were a foretaste of what was inevitably to come.

Lough Swilly crews, under the able direction of traffic manager, Connell Diver, did sterling work during and after events such as the Battle of the Bogside in 1969, or the British Army's Operation Motorman, ferrying load after load of traumatised Bogside and Creggan children, to safety over the border into Donegal. The Swilly was not found wanting when it was needed most.

It was probably a bit mad to go to Derry as a young buck of 23 in July 1974, but I did phone my fiancée successfully and we got married the following year and are still going strong. I saw the Swilly HQ in action, and, above all, was saved from incarceration by the official letterhead of the Londonderry & Lough Swilly Railway Company.

I still have that letter. It was my Lough Swilly get-out-of-jail free card….

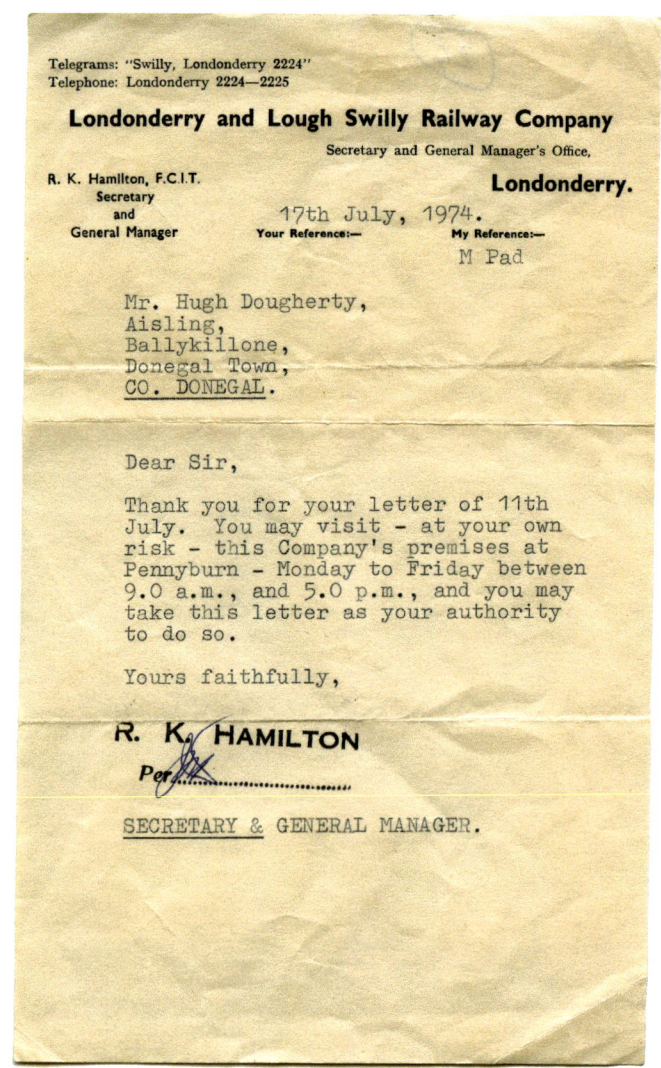

My Lough Swilly get-out-of-jail-free card! The letter that stood between me and arrest…   *Hugh Dougherty*

FRONT

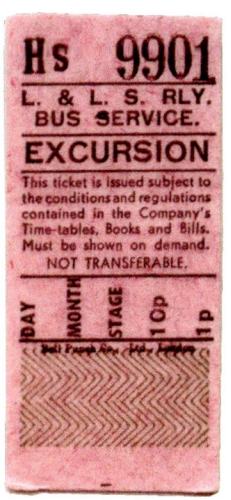    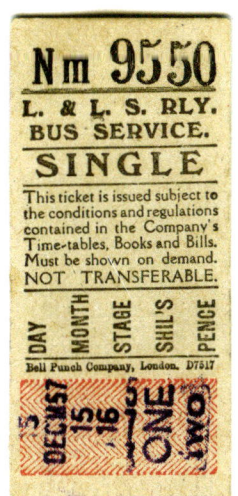 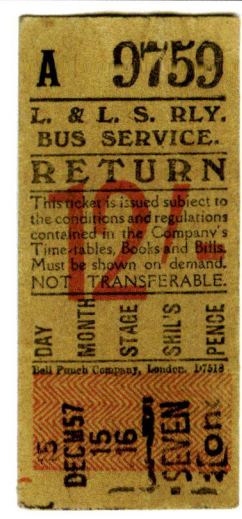

    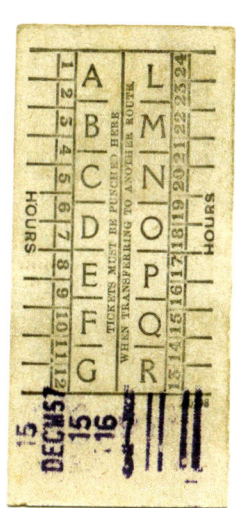 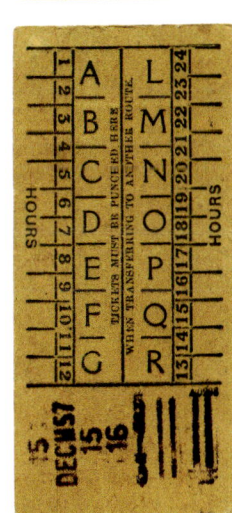

BACK

Some of the tickets that I was given as a souvenir by the manager.   *Hugh Dougherty.*

Cashelnagor, looking toward Burtonport with Errigal rearing skywards. The highest station on the extension from Letterkenny, this is a remote spot!
Hugh Dougherty.

CASHELNAGOR SERIOUSLY SEEKING THE SWILLY

There's nothing more redolent of the great days of the Swilly's Letterkenny & Burtonport Extension Railway, that scenic and sinewy, 50-mile line, opened in 1903, than the atmospherically-remote, Cashelnagor Station.

Built deep in the fastness of the bogs between Falcarragh and Gweedore, Cashelnagor, despite its remote location, looking out towards the Derryveagh Mountains and the impressive bulk of Errigal, this station did a brisk trade in its time, with goods and passengers keeping the staff busy up until the closure of the line in 1947.

I'd marvelled at the station's location, five miles by road from Gortahork, and the nearest Lough Swilly bus route, and tried to work out how to get to it, to soak up its atmosphere, but, it evaded me. That was, until 2019, when my wife and I stayed there thanks to its reincarnation as a holiday let.

The station opened in 1903 as the highest point, at 420 feet above sea level, of the Letterkenny & Burtonport Extension Railway, built by the British Government to boost fishing at Burtonport, as part of Lord Balfour's plans to kill Home Rule, as he said, with kindness.

But the line had a more sinister purpose. That was to link West Donegal with Derry, so that thousands could sail for Scotland and the United States, releasing pressure on the land of West Donegal, and cutting unrest and demands for Home Rule. Some might claim that it was ethnic cleansing by rail.

Between 1903 and 1947, the Londonderry & Lough Swilly Railway served Cashelnagor, with two trains daily to Derry and Burtonport carrying herring, goods of all sorts, and, crucially, thousands of migrating local people from along the line, to new lives. In the wooden-seated carriages were seasonal "tattie howkers", for lowland Scottish farms potato harvesting. Children, as young as 14, travelled to the Letterkenny Hiring Fair, to be snapped up, almost as in a slave market, by the rich, Protestant farmers of the fertile Lagan area, to work for a full year away from home.

The forebears of thousands of members of the Scottish, Irish diaspora began their journey here, from Cashelnagor, and that atmosphere can be tapped into today. Just stand on the restored platform by the abandoned track bed, and you can almost hear the whistle of a heavy steam train, drawn by number 12, the line's mighty 4-8-0 tender locomotive, specially built for the job, forging up the gradient from Gweedore, before sad farewells take place and carriage doors slam shut on life among the hills of Donegal.

In its day, the station survived the traumas of the War of Independence, the Civil War and partition, and it was also a popular, social, meeting place of an evening, as local young people gathered to welcome the train, and to see who got on and off. One station master, an Orangeman, was hounded out of the station by locals, after his son allegedly derailed a train, and, after closure, the last station master and his family stayed on in the now-trainless station, then still owned by the Swilly, until 1954, after which it was abandoned.

But, phoenix-like, Cashelnagor came back to life, briefly in 1992, when the BBC cosmetically restored the main buildings to shoot scenes for *The Railway Station Man*, starring Julie Christie and Donald Sutherland, released in 1993. But, otherwise the station began to return to nature, until Neil Tee, an English railway buff, bought it in 2005, and began limited restoration.

But it wasn't until 2017, that the station's fortunes really changed, for local couple, Gavin and Josephine Kelly, bought the semi-ruin, and, over the next year, they not only rebuilt the station, but restored it faithfully, too, capturing all of its character while putting in electricity, central heating and plumbing, and fitting it out as two holiday lets.

The larger one, accommodating up to eight people, is in the station master's house, with a turf fire, kitchen, dining room, sitting room and two bedrooms, one en-suite and a bathroom with vintage bath, while the smaller, the former ticket office and waiting room, can accommodate four.

Everything has been done tastefully and as close as possible to the original, so that comfort is king as the winds, and sometimes, the rains of Donegal rage outside, as we found that June (!), giving a real impression of what life must have been like for the station master and his family, between trains, in this remote and bleak spot.

There are lovely touches, such as framed Lough Swilly Railway Letterkenny Hiring Fair and timetable posters, an authentic L&LSR cast iron sign warning against leaving gates open to allow livestock to wander on the line, while period lampposts complete the illusion that a train might just call again sometime soon.

Said Josephine. "We're very conscious of the fact that we're custodians of a significant piece of local, railway heritage, as well as providing quality, holiday accommodation."

If you do want to explore the railway heritage of Donegal, this is an excellent location, and there's even access to a railway walk on the old track bed to Falcarragh Station, and on to lonely and lovely Lough Agher, below the great bulk of Muckish Mountain. That's a walk that will open your eyes to the challenges that contractor Pauling, and the men who built this line, faced as it fought its way through a wildly romantic, but unforgiving landscape. You'll marvel at the quality of the engineering, especially the bridges still standing today. You can almost see a Swilly train battling the elements to bring the outside world to West Donegal by rail, changing the way of life for thousands in the process.

But lift your eyes from the tracks towards the magnificence of Errigal and the Derryveaghs, or drive out to the coast at Gortahork. You can visit the enchanting Bloody Foreland, head up to Falcarragh and its magnificent strand, or make tracks for Magherarorty Strand and the coast line of the Rosses. This is Lough Swilly Railway territory, a fact that local people are waking up to more and more, keen both to preserve the heritage as well as recycling relics of the railway positively for today's tourism and leisure market.

There are plans to develop the entire Lough Swilly Railway track bed from Derry to Burtonport as a greenway for walking and cycling, linking sections already completed at Burtonport,

The station displays a poster for special hiring fair trains in 1934.

Hugh Dougherty

Seeking and finding the Swilly! Hugh on the platform at Cashelnagor in June 2019 during his stay at the atmospheric station. *Hugh Dougherty*

Walking towards Falcarragh on the railway track bed with one of the original bridges still carrying traffic today. *Hugh Dougherty*

Creeslough and Falcarragh, so, Cashelnagor Station could be connected, once again by the railway that brought it to the hills of Donegal in the early years of last century.

Just down the track, there's the remains of Crolly and Gweedore Stations, with the track bed clearly visible, while down at Kincasslagh Road, you can see the memorial to the rescue of two local men from the clutches of the British Army in 1918. At Burtonport, where, sadly, the station buildings were demolished, there's a display in the community and heritage centre on the Swilly which includes a superb 4mm scale model of the station by talented Irish narrow gauge modeller, Alan Gee, and donated by him to the community. There's also a restored platelayer's bogie, which used to traverse a siding retained at Burtonport after closure for fish transport along the quayside.

Back at Cashelnagor, I did ensure that the station welcomed its first Lough Swilly train since 1947, even if it was in the shape of my own 4mm scale model of 4-6-0T number 2. The real loco was built by Andrew Barclay in Kilmarnock for the Burtonport line, and I also brought an L&BER wagon and a brake van. Placed on the edge of the platform with the station building behind, the train did look quite authentic and recalled the great days of Cashenagor Station, now restored to its former old glory.

It's a must see for anyone seriously seeking the Swilly.

The first train back at Cashelnagor since the line closed. Hugh's 00n3 Lough Swilly railway models sit on the platform. The name board has been restored. Cashelnagor comes from two Irish words, Caishel, a ring fort, and corr, a small hill, so people lived here long before the railway arrived in 1903.

Hugh Dougherty

You can walk on the track bed to Falcarragh Station, the next station up the line towards Derry.

Hugh Dougherty

Seeking the Swilly – Innishowen

It's 08.00 on a dull, Tuesday 27th July, 1982, and I'm standing outside our Ballyliffin holiday home on the village main street, waiting for the Swilly to Buncrana and Derry. The bus has left Carndonagh Station on the rail replacement service, – the line shut in 1935 – at 7.40, and it picks me up bang on time. I buy my insert Setright card ticket, headed "L&LSRly – Bus Service", through to Derry, from the friendly driver, now working one-man, following the loss of his conductor in an economy drive. The conductor is still remembered, however, by a traditional, leather cash bag, slung across the control panel, and used by the driver for his cash and change.

There are only two other passengers on board fleet number 228, a Willowbrook-bodied Leyland Leopard, new to Maidstone and District in 1968, and transferred to the Swilly in 1981, as part of a covert, financial rescue deal by the Irish Government. That was via CIE, when, once again, the L&LSR was in dire financial straits, and seeking help, so Dublin aid had to be disguised, as the company's HQ was over the border in Derry.

As we set off for Clonmany, passing Ballyliffin Station, we see sections of railway track bed and two crossing keeper's cottages on the way, and, so far, no more passengers. But, in and past Clonmany, the bus fairly fills up with girls heading for sewing work at Buncrana's Fruit of the Loom factory. This is a Swilly commuter bus in a very rural setting, and business is brisk, as the driver welcomes all his regulars by name and cancels the right section of weekly tickets, using a traditional railway-style set of nippers, chained to the dashboard and clearly dating from train days.

We're right on time into Buncrana's characterful St Mary's Road bus station, built in 1950, closer to the centre, as the railway station was situated almost out of the town, and I had plenty of time to look around as I waited for the 09.00 Derry, over the original route of the Swilly's railway line, of 1861. Buncrana, known colloquially in Derry as 'Budgen' was a significant, Swilly traffic generator right from the start, with bus and rail excursions bringing in the cash as Derry folk made for the town's seaside delights on the shores of Lough Swilly.

During the Second World War hordes of off-duty, British Navy sailors from Derry naval base, at Lisahally, disguised in civvies, crammed into the Swilly trains to enjoy Buncrana's lack of rationing and other unspecified pleasures (!), and there is evidence that the late Prince Philip, whenever his ship put into Derry between patrols in the Atlantic, also travelled on narrow gauge rails to and from the seaside town.

Royalty was no stranger to the Swilly. On 28th July 1903, the Crown had travelled over the same line, when King Edward VII and Queen Alexandra had sailed to Buncrana Pier, boarded the Swilly train at Buncrana Station, and travelled in a special Royal Saloon, hired from the Ballymena & Larne section of the Belfast & Northern Counties Railway, for the day, to Derry. There Edward presented the city with one of the hundreds of trademark busts of himself that he seemed to leave wherever he visited – you can see the Derry one, today in the Guildhall – and went back to Buncrana on the Royal Train, with the Swilly renaming the locomotive, 4-6-2T, number 7, *Edward VII*, for the occasion, before he sailed off up Lough Foyle.

That sense of continuity with the company's rich history was in my mind as we left Buncrana bang on 09.00, on another British ex-pat Leopard, in the then-current red-and-cream livery. We passed the impressive railway station, still extant today, as one of many railway buildings surviving along the course of the Innishowen line, and, although the Royal, Train, and indeed all trains, had long gone by 1982, I had hoped to travel in style on a Swilly double decker, so characteristic of the busy Derry – Buncrana route, into Derry, but had to make do with a lowly single decker.

Still, timekeeping was good, as we picked up a fair number of shoppers heading for Derry, passing the site of Fahan Station, again, around today, and now a successful, railway-themed

Crowds throng Ballyliffin platform on a summer Sunday in the 1920s as their train, hauled by one of the large 4-8-4 tank locos, arrives to take them home to Derry after a day on Pollan Strand. They had left Derry at 11.30, after Mass (!) arrived in Ballyliffin at 1.00pm, and boarded this train at 8.00 pm., arriving back in Derry at 9.30pm. Quite a day out!

Sean Crawford, the Bigger and McDonald Collection.

Ballyliffin Station today. It's hard to believe that it was once so busy.

Hugh Dougherty

On the very spot where the train crossed the road, Dennis Dart 481 runs through Ballyliffin for Carndonagh on a July day in 2008. *Hugh Dougherty*

restaurant, while you could also make out the course of the line heading for Tooban Junction, and Burnfoot and Bridgend. But, as we approached the Customs, who seemed to have lost interest that day, apart from a cursory look inside the bus, it was then time to stop for the British Army checkpoint at Coshquin.

The really remarkable thing was that some local lads, all long hair and flares, that is of the trouser variety, heading into Derry, were lounging under an overhang of the main watchtower, from whose upper window a squaddie was swapping banter with them, before the bus stopped beside them, as though using an official bus shelter. They crowded on, and that was it, a great contrast to what I'd experienced back in 1974.

Although, the late Canon John McKegney, a former chairman of the Railway Preservation Society of Ireland, who worked as a Swilly conductor during his student days in the early 1970s, did tell me that on the last Friday night bus from Buncrana, the top deck could get just a wee bit wild.

"I remember we were stopped at the checkpoint and an earnest, young British soldier boarded and told me that he intended to check upstairs where the usual, riotous, mobile party was underway. I told him to go ahead and try, but that it would be at his own risk. He poked his head up the stairs, took one look, retreated, and said with a look of relief on his face: 'OK, on you go!' As I belled the bus away, I wondered what his chances would have been if he'd gone ahead. I did note that his more experienced colleagues stayed off the bus and just nodded to us to go on, as they usually did on that last run. I'm sure he learned in time."

Not that the Customs weren't stricter in earlier times, with smuggling on the Swilly an art-form. Conductor Jackie Donaghy recorded on the TV4 programme *Bealach na mBusanna*, shown in 2012: "It was the time when Crombie overcoats were popular and I brought them to order across the border from Derry for people in Donegal. It was easy to hide them under the long, bench seats in the double deckers. I made about £10 out of that. Mind you, I had done some favours for the Customs boys themselves!" And, on the same programme, some now very respectable Donegal ladies recalled with plenty of mirth how they would go down on the Swilly bus to buy underwear which was cheaper in the north, don the lot under their dresses, to get past the Customs, and then hang select items out of the windows the minute the bus crossed the border to wind up the Customs men! Smuggling on the Swilly could be risqué. An undercover operation, you might say!

But, my Swilly trip down to Derry that July day was a mission with a purpose, as our Reliant Robin estate car, yes, really, we were poor in those days – well, a van with windows, and back seat added – had broken a rear spring in a trench dug across the road at Drunkeen by Telecon Eireann, the day before, on our way back from a visit to my friends at the former County Donegal Railway office at Stranorlar. Thankfully, the brake pipe survived intact, we – that is our sons Hugh, then 6, and Brendan, 3, and my wife Patricia, expecting number three – were able to limp back all the way to Ballyliffin. The fact that a CIE Leopard broke one of its springs on the Letterkenny service at the same spot the following day was little comfort.

Ballyliffin's Devlin's Ponderosa Motors, declared that they could get us back on the road, if I could get a spring, as Mr Devlin had served his time with a Reliant garage in England. A call to Ireland's only Reliant dealer in Belfast, ascertained that they had a spring and could get it to Derry by Ulsterbus parcels, as long as I could get a money order to them right away.

That involved a dash to Clonmany Post Office, negotiating the hurdles resulting from the Republic's use of Punts, introduced in 1979, which also caused a headache for the Swilly as it was taking fares in both Punts and Sterling. I then had to wire a money order across the border. Thankfully, the dealer confirmed that he had the money, and that the spring would arrive that afternoon in Derry. You forget how complex all that could be in those long-lost, pre-mobile phone and internet days.

Once I'd picked the spring up at Foyle Road Bus Station's Ulsterbus parcels office – remember when bus stations had such facilities – I'd time to kill before joining the 17.15, busy commuter service to Buncrana, then transferring to the 17.55 for Ballyliffin, so

Scenic Swilly, an ex-CIE Leyland Leopard runs past the strip fields outside Ballyliffin on its way from Carndonagh to Buncrana in July 1981.
Hugh Dougherty

I ordered a birthday cake for my wife who'd be 32 the next day, and carried that, and the spring, back with me all the way home by Swilly bus. The exercise wasn't helped by the fact that the cake was boxed, large and gooey and the spring was getting heavier as I had to stand on the packed single decker Leopard as far as Fahan, before the loading eased. I did enjoy a chat with a Glasgow Donegal man, complete with a vintage 1950s suitcase, who was heading home on holidays to Carndonagh. There he was: an example of the traditional, Swilly Scotchie traffic in person, but, by 1982, just a bit of a throwback with his suitcase in hand.

The L&LSR was still doing good business on the Buncrana road in those days, despite underlying financial difficulties with its more remote routes, and it would survive another 32 years before the end came. My experience, that day, was of smart running, well-turned-out drivers in uniform, parcel and newspaper traffic alive and well, with the mid-week edition of the *Derry Journal* was being carried on the service for distribution, by a Swilly factotum, to shops along the way.

It was good to experience the service over the original route of the company between Derry and Buncrana, while the Buncrana – Carndonagh service exactly mirrored the timetable to the trains it had replaced, with three services, morning, noon and evening, in each direction.

Over the years since, we've holidayed in Innishowen many times, the peninsula, after all, being home to the Dougherty clan, and, up until the closure of the company in 2014, the Swilly was a constant presence. I also sought out the remains of the Carndonagh line, and delved into local history sources to find out about its life and times.

As we stayed beside Ballyliffin Station, still there today as a private house, I found out all I could. The arrival of the railway transformed the village, as trains brought holidaymakers and day trippers to its superb Pollan Bay Strand, a hotel and guesthouses opened, and the *Derry Journal*, in 1906, five years after the Carndonagh line opened, described Ballyliffin as 'The New Blackpool'!

Thankfully, that transformation didn't happen, but in 1927, the railway had to extend the station platform to accommodate the popular, eight coach, summer, Sunday, excursion trains from Carndonagh and Derry. The Derry train was often drawn by one of the massive 4-8-4 tank locos, built for the lengthy trip from Derry to Burtonport, and not otherwise usually seen on the Carn line, so important was this traffic. It's hard to imagine all of that today, as the station sleeps, but the line's presence is recalled on a public information, heritage panel, just outside its gates, stating that the Swilly, its trains and its station, changed the fortunes of Ballyliffin forever. The village remained a popular destination for Lough Swilly bus day tours for many years after, and still attracts many visitors today.

Interestingly, we had an elderly nun in our parish in Glasgow, then a little Donegal in its own right, in the 1980s. She came from Ballyliffin and more than recalled the railway in the early 1930s, when she was a girl. "We would travel on the train to Carn," she told me. "Mammy would tell me and the rest of the family to hide under the seats in the compartment to avoid paying, and the adults would hide us with their legs. But I can recall Mr Whyte, the manager himself, coming to Ballyliffin all the way from his office in Derry to read the riot act and threaten dire penalties to anyone caught dodging paying their fare as the railway was losing a fortune. That stopped it for a while, but I do remember trying to avoid paying on the school train to Rashenny!"

You can still view the station house at Rashenny that the good sister tried to avoid buying a ticket to. It's now a private home and Ireland's most northerly railway station. The station buildings at Carndonagh, sold off by the Swilly after being used for bus and lorry traffic, long after the 1935 railway closure, are not just intact, but sensitively maintained by its current owners, a fish processing company. When I called in a couple of years ago, there was a framed Swilly timetable up on the wall, a picture of the station in its heyday and the friendly man at the desk told me with some pride that his grandfather had been the station master, simply proving that if you seek out the Swilly, you will still find it today.

Seeking the Swilly on two wheels! Hugh at Clonmany Station which is very much intact.
Patricia Dougherty

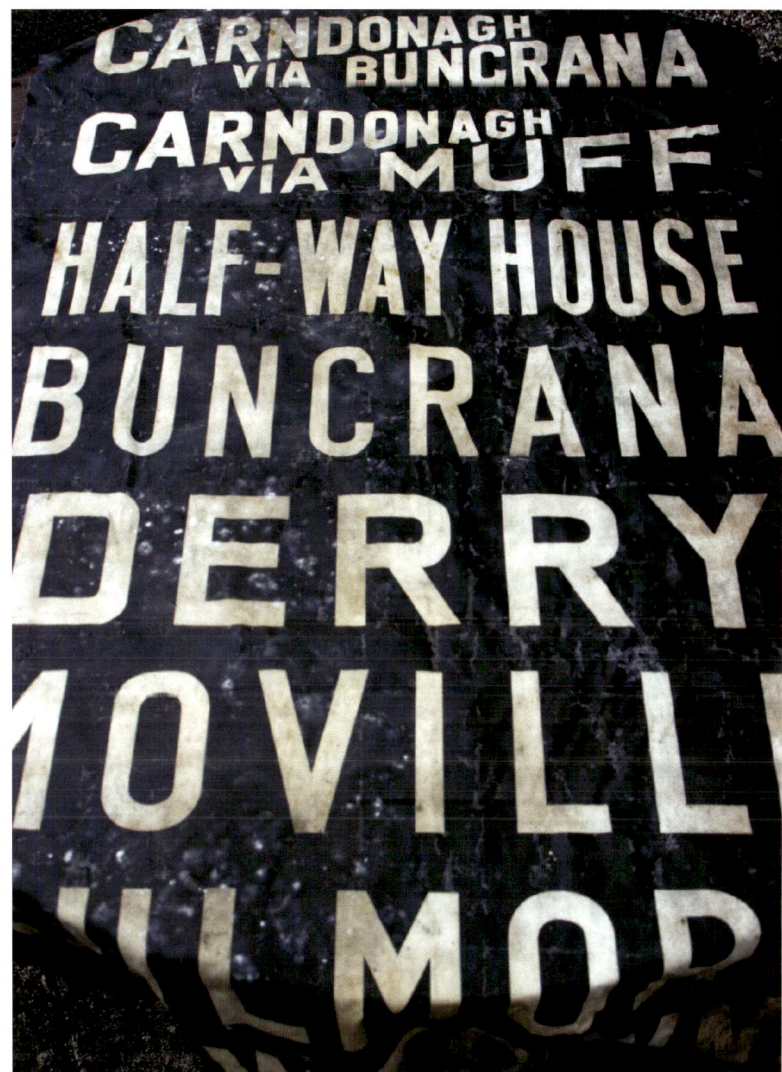

Blind date! Where a Swilly bus could take you as shown on this destination blind. *Hugh Dougherty*

Down the line towards Buncrana, there's much to see, too, at Clonmany Station, with its high-quality, cut stone buildings, and courses of yellow, Ruabon brick, as specified by the Board of Trade at the building of the line, still there today. The station house and booking office, built to the same design as Glenties and Letterkenny stations, is in use as a dwelling house. You can also see the water tower, its tank made of cast iron by a Derry foundry, and platforms. Clonmany was the passing point on the single-tracked Carn line, while it was a busy place with British military traffic before and during the First World War, as there were several army training camps in the area around the village. Strange to imagine that this now, slumbering station was the departure point by Swilly train, for hundreds of soldiers making their way after training outside Clonmany, to the killing fields of Flanders, while it also saw a healthy traffic in both horses, jockeys and spectators, during the Clonmany Races down at Tullagh Bay.

Innishowen was a major centre of Swilly activity, and that's often forgotten, as people tend to associate the company very much with its epic railway to Burtonport. But, in Innishowen, the coming of the Carn line stimulated fishing, shirt making, agriculture and tourism, while, in bus and lorry days, the company provided services up both sides of the peninsula, and, famously, right up to Malin Head, Ireland's most northerly point. It's the piece of geography that makes a nonsense of the term 'Northern Ireland', Malin Head being famously, very definitely, located in the political 'South'!

The story is still told locally of the regular bus crew on the Malin Head run, who picked up a mysterious passenger, definitely not one of their regulars, during The Emergency, as the Second World War was known in the Republic. He boarded at Malin Head terminus, was strangely dressed, spoke English with a foreign accent, and tendered exactly the right amount, much to the conductor's amazement, for his fare to Malin Town.

There, he alighted at the Malin Cash Stores in the Diamond, and when the bus crew returned on their way north again, he boarded, this time, laden down with plenty of food, paid his fare again, and

The Ghosts of Tooban Junction's unique signal, with two arms on one post, facing different platform faces, as sculpted by John McCarron.

John McCarron

alighted at Malin Head, disappearing over the hill towards the sea. Not only had this mysterious man known the Lough Swilly bus timetable and fares, but he had even known where the nearest shop was. When the crew reported the episode, they were told by Gardai that he'd most likely been off a German U-boat, seen lying off Malin Head by some local people, and had taken his chance to get some fresh food for the crew. How the Kriegsmarine knew Swilly bus times and fares, remains one of the great mysteries of the Second World War!

Still in Innishowen, you'll now be hard-put to make out the once-picturesque Meedoran Viaduct, clearly visible from the road as late as the 1990s, just south of Clonmany, because of unchecked tree growth. Buncrana sculptor, John McCarron, is keen to free the bridge from its vegetation, just as he's planning to build a replica Swilly platelayer's bogie, used for maintaining the line, for display at the North Pole pub, which, was, of course, Drumfries Station, north of Buncrana. He's also keen to rebuild the now-derelict Burnfoot Station, as a Lough Swilly Railway heritage centre.

John, well-known as the sculptor of the Glasgow Famine Memorial, has already put his ideas into practice at Tooban Junction, where the Buncrana and Letterkenny lines bisected, and has put the once-busy station back on the map with a replica of the two-way signal that used to stand at the end of the platform, along with a see-through display board, showing the real signal and train waiting by it, taken in 1953, just before the closure of the line.

Known as The Ghosts of Tooban Junction, the accurate and atmospheric metal sculpture is reachable from Inch Wildfowl Reserve, and has helped pinpoint the exact location of the junction which faded away into the undergrowth after the track was lifted. John's work has helped keep the memory of the Swilly alive on its home ground, something that the sculptor feels is very important today.

And it was Innishowen, too, that threw up another memory of the Swilly, on the eastern side of the peninsula, in Moville, one-time calling station for liners going from Glasgow to New York.

Moville was home of Viscount Montgomery of Second World War fame and an important Lough Swilly bus terminus and staging point, as, despite several abortive schemes, which included a 3ft gauge electric railway, à la Manx Electric, Moville never did manage to get its own railway.

Up until 2014, when the Swilly went bust, you would always find a LSR bus lying over on the main street, where the company used to have a bus office, between runs. The town was once served by double-deckers, some of which went as far north as Innishowen Head. Moville had an indefinable Swilly spirit about it, despite the fact that it was a bus-only town. It was no surprise, then when, in summer 2022, I noticed a local shop selling Lough Swilly bus posters, depicting a Swilly bus threading through the Hills of Donegal, with what looked like Muckish Mountain in the background.

In reality, it was a doctored Ulster Transport Authority poster, with the bus altered to show 'Moville" on its screen, a Lough Swilly logo placed on its side, and a 1950s, 'IH' Donegal registration added. Despite that, I simply had to have one, and, for just two Euros, one was mine. As the lady who sold me it, said: "We do miss the Swilly buses. They did a lot for Moville and brought thousands of visitors and Derry day-trippers here. These are selling very well."

And, for Innishowen, there's still-extant Ballymagan Station, north of Buncrana to mention, and the remains of the viaduct over the Crana River, just outside Buncrana, on the way north, too. So, take your time and arm yourself with a copy of the Donegal Railway Heritage Trail, produced by Donegal Railway Heritage Museum, and you should be able to seek out the Swilly for yourself.

All these years later, I'm still seeking out the Swilly in Innishowen, our ancestral homeland – my wife and I often do our Swilly searching along the tracks on our bikes. Who knows what might turn up next on our searches for remains of this once-great railway company, sadly, now consigned to history, but, definitely not forgotten in the areas of Donegal it once served so well.

The Swilly poster from Moville, a Lough Swilly town if ever there was one, despite being on Lough Foyle! *Hugh Dougherty collection*

The surviving Swilly coach and crane truck, safe and sound within the Foyle Valley Railway Museum. *Hugh Dougherty*

SEEK AND YOU WILL FIND...

It's sad that no locomotives and few pieces of rolling stock have survived, but you can still seek out a genuine Swilly coach, number 17, preserved in Derry's Foyle Valley Railway Museum, along with the company's rail crane.

The crane's mounted on an underframe with axle boxes lettered L&BER, the initials of the legendary Letterkenny & Burtonport Extension Railway. A 'No Trespassing' notice completes the Foyle Road Swilly collection.

What is thought to be a LSR wagon was discovered near to Letterkenny 2022, and is being assessed by Donegal Railway Museum, home to Newtoncunninghan Signal Box, which does duty, so as to speak, as the museum's toilet! Newton's ticket office window has also been rescued and is on show in the museum, along with a display board on the Swilly, a company Setright ticket machine and examples of LSR bus timetables.

Also, at Donegal Town quayside, is the restored crane from Fahan Railway Pier. It was spirited away from its Innishowen home, where it had stood for close on 100 years, in 2022, by Donegal County Council, after the pier had become unsafe. Fully restored to its old glory, its transfer to County Donegal Railways territory, didn't go down well with the West Innishowen Historical Society, which wanted the crane kept beside Fahan Railway Station, as a key part of the village's railway heritage.

There are displays on the railway in Dunfanaghy Workhouse Museum and at Newmills Corn Mill, outside Letterkenny, while Letterkenny Bus Station, the former CDR station for the town, the Swilly's having been demolished in the 1980s to make way for a shopping centre, is home to a display of the CDR and Swilly trains, thanks to a local heritage group. The town's Station Hotel, built on the site of Oldtown Station, first stop on the Burtonport line, has a fine mural of 4-6-0T number 3, heading a Burtonport train, crossing the still-extant Swilly bridge close to the hotel, while Donegal County Museum, also in Letterkenny, has railway company material, too.

The Londonderry & Lough Swilly Railway shares with two other Irish railway companies, the honour of having a piece of music written about it. Percy French immortalised the narrow gauge West Clare Railway, with *Are ye right there Michael, are ye right?*, while Big Tom and the Mainliners wrote and performed The *GNR Steam Train*. Phil Coulter wrote *The Lough Swilly Railway* for his *Lake of Shadows* album, while Celtic Thunder perform a rousing version of the atmospheric piece as part of the group's repertoire. You can almost hear the clatter of carriage wheels on rail joints by the shores of Lough Swilly in the music!

Two 4mm scale, Lough Swilly bus models have been produced in the shape of an Original Omnibus Company, Letterkenny-bound, Leyland Leopard, number 244, while Oxford Diecast has a model of Leyland Royal Tiger Coach, number 101. Its tiny screen carries the destination 'Malin Head', the most famous Lough Swilly terminus of all. Several model railway manufacturers produce kits of Swilly locomotives, coaches and wagons, but the bus models remain the only 'ready-to-run' models of company rolling stock.

The Oxford Diecast Leyland Royal Tiger is for Malin Head.

Oxford Diecast

But, taking the honours in the still-running category, is the only operating, full scale, piece of Londonderry & Lough Swilly Railway rolling stock, in the shape of bus fleet number 452, Alexander-bodied, Bristol RELL6G, owned and run by Manchester-based, Belfast exile, Tommy Mitchell. New to Ulsterbus in 1984, the bus was bought by the Swilly in 2004 and ran, mainly on school services, until 2007, when it was saved from scrapping by enthusiasts. It eventually passed to Tommy, who restored the bus fully, in 2021. Resplendent in its Lough Swilly livery, it delights visitors to North West of England bus rallies, and, as Tommy says, draws plenty of interest from Derry and Donegal exiles, who, recognising the bus, regale him with memories of their Lough Swilly journeys back home.

If you want to hear what a Lough Swilly loco whistle sounded like, echoing off the hills and remoteness of the Burtonport

Swilly magnificence in miniature. The sheer power and bulk of 4-8-0 mumber 12 impresses even as a scale model.

High Leigh Miniature Railway

The back of Tommy Mitchell's Lough Swilly 452.   *Daniel Tartaglia*

Extension line, make tracks for the Cavan & Leitrim Railway at Dromod, where the line's 0-6-0T, *Nancy* has been fitted with a whistle off one of the Swilly 'giants', the massive 4-8-4T engines built for the Burtonport road.

Lastly, if you want to see a Swilly steam engine in action, you can do just that at the High Leigh Miniature Railway in Cheshire, where a superb, 7¼ inch-scale, live steam model of 4-8-0 number 12, has been built by Bob Butler. Resplendent in Swilly green it's as impressive as the prototype, and a living reminder that the L&LSR served the people of Donegal, so faithfully and well for so many decades, What a pity it is that number 12 itself was scrapped in 1953. Who knows, we might have been able to see the real thing in action on a length of preserved track, perhaps, somewhere in Donegal.

We can but dream and keep seeking the Swilly……